Pebble® Plus

Backyard Birds

Goldfinches

by Lisa J. Amstutz

Consulting Editor:
Gail Saunders-Smith, PhD

Consultant: André Dhondt,
Morgens Professor of Ornithology,
Cornell Laboratory of Ornithology

CAPSTONE PRESS
a capstone imprint

Pebble Plus is published by Capstone Press,
1710 Roe Crest Drive, North Mankato, Minnesota 56003
www.capstonepub.com

Library of Congress Cataloging-in-Publication Data

Amstutz, Lisa J.

Goldfinches / by Lisa J. Amstutz.

pages cm. — (Pebble plus. Backyard birds)

Summary: "Simple text and full-color photographs introduce goldfinches"—Provided by publisher.

Audience: Ages 5-7

Audience: K to grade 3

Includes bibliographical references and index.

ISBN 978-1-4914-6108-2 (library binding)

ISBN 978-1-4914-6112-9 (paperback)

ISBN 978-1-4914-6116-7 (eBook PDF)

1. Goldfinches—Juvenile literature. I. Title.

QL696.P246A47 2016

598.8'85—dc23

2015001327

Editorial Credits

Elizabeth R. Johnson, editor; Bobbie Nuytten, designer;
Svetlana Zhurkin, media researcher; Tori Abraham, production specialist

Photo Credits

Getty Images: Anthony Mercieca, 19, Gary Meszaros, 17; Minden Pictures: Jan Luit, 13; Shutterstock:
Danussa, 4 and throughout, Gregg Williams, cover (inset), 1 (inset), Iriana Shiyan, cover (back), 1
(back), 2—3, 24, Kelly Nelson, 9, Lonnie Gorsline, 11, Lorraine Hudgins, 7, Nancy Bauer, 15, rck_953,
5, Tony Campbell, 21

Note to Parents and Teachers

The Backyard Birds set supports national curriculum standards for science related to
life science and ecosystems. This book describes and illustrates American goldfinches.
The images support early readers in understanding the text. The repetition of words
and phrases helps early readers learn new words. This book also introduces early
readers to subject-specific vocabulary words, which are defined in the Glossary
section. Early readers may need assistance to read some words and to use the Table of
Contents, Glossary, Read More, Internet Sites, Critical Thinking Using the Common
Core, and Index sections of the book.

Printed in the United States of America in North Mankato, Minnesota.
032015   008823CGF15

Table of Contents

All About Goldfinches

American goldfinches dip
and soar as they fly.
They sing a cheery song.
Per-chick-o-ree!

Goldfinches are small birds.

They are about 4 to 5.5 inches

(11 to 14 centimeters) long.

That's about the length

of your hand.

The birds molt twice a year.

In summer, males are bright yellow.

Females are dull yellow.

In winter, both are light brown.

Goldfinches perch on thistle plants.

They pick out seeds with their sharp beaks.

Seeds are their favorite food.

Goldfinch Homes

Goldfinches live in North America. They are found in fields and towns. They live in large flocks.

The female makes a nest in summer. She uses bits of plants to make a soft cup.

She ties the nest to a branch with spider silk.

The Life of a Goldfinch

The female lays two to seven light blue eggs. She sits on them to keep them warm. The chicks hatch in two weeks.

The parents bring food
to their young.
The chicks grow fast.
Soon they are ready
to leave the nest.

You can invite goldfinches
to your yard. Just put out
some thistle seeds.
These busy birds are
fun to watch!

Glossary

chick—a young bird

flock—a group of animals that live, travel, and eat together

hatch—to break out of an egg

molt—when a bird molts, old feathers are shed while new feathers grow to replace them

nest—a place to lay eggs and bring up young

perch—to sit or stand on a branch or on the edge of something, often high up

thistle—a wild plant that has sharp points on its leaves and purple, yellow, or white flowers; goldfinches eat thistle seeds

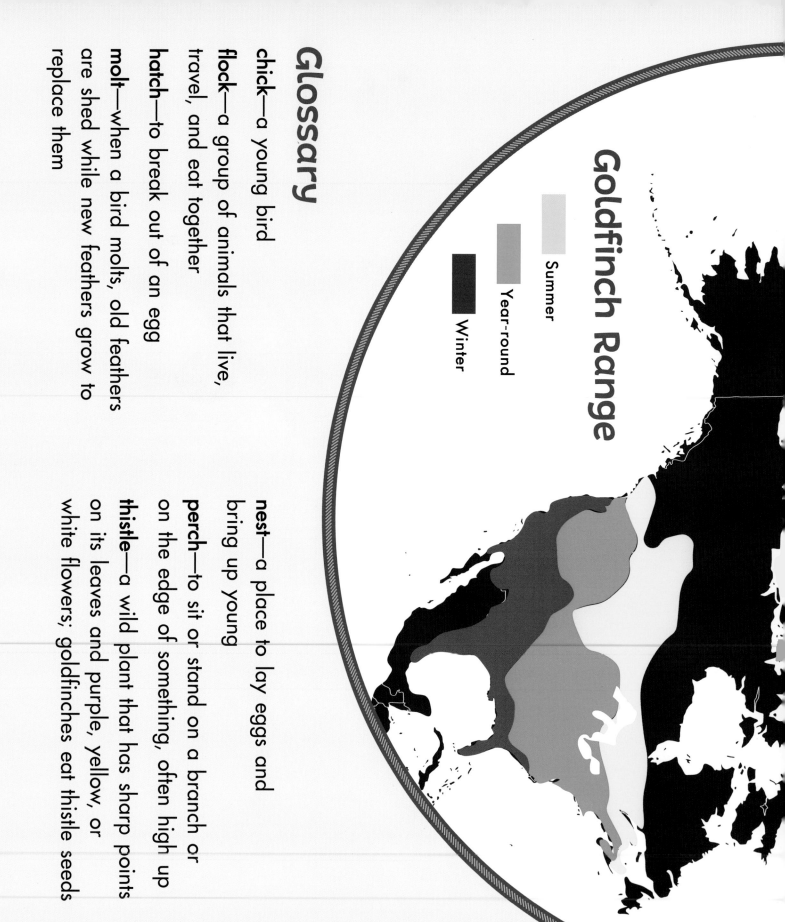

Goldfinch Range

Summer

Year-round

Winter

Read More

Alderfer, Jonathan. *National Geographic Kids Bird Guide of North America.* Washington, D.C.: National Geographic, 2013.

Kurki, Kim. *National Wildlife Federation's World of Birds: A Beginner's Guide.* Black Dog & Leventhal Publishers, 2014.

Russo, Monica. *Birdology: 30 Activities and Observations for Exploring the World of Birds.* Chicago: Chicago Review Press, 2015.

Internet Sites

FactHound offers a safe, fun way to find Internet sites related to this book. All of the sites on FactHound have been researched by our staff.

Here's all you do:

Visit *www.facthound.com*

Type in this code: 9781491461082

Super-cool stuff!

Check out projects, games and lots more at **www.capstonekids.com**

Critical Thinking
Using the Common Core

1. Goldfinches are small birds. What is a simple way to show the size of a goldfinch? (Key Ideas and Details)

2. Goldfinches are different colors during the year. How does that happen? (Key Ideas and Details)

3. Look at the photo on page 21. How can you invite goldfinches to your yard? (Integration of Knowledge and Ideas)

Index

colors, 8

eggs, 16

flocks, 12

food, 10, 18, 20

habitats, 12

nests, 14

size, 6

songs, 4

young, 18

Word Count: 182
Grade: 1
Early-Intervention Level: 13